KWANZAA

Everything You Always Wanted To Know But Didn't Know Where To Ask

Revised Edition

Cedric McClester

GUMBS & THOMAS, Publishers *New York*

Credits

Cover Design: *Bob Gumbs*

Cover Painting: *Ademola Olugebefola*

Text Illustrations: *Abdullah Aziz*, p. 28; *Yvette Crawford-Jenkins*, pp. 18, 18, 24, 25; *Dindga McCannon*, p. xii; *Ademola Olugebefola*, pp. 6, 7, 8, 15; *Abdul Rahman*, p. 32; *Charlotte Richardson*, p. 4; *James Sepyo*, p. 16.

Text Photos: *Kwame Brathwaite* and *Bob Gumbs*, p. 21.

Copyright © 1990, 1985 by Gumbs & Thomas, Publishers, Inc. and Cedric McClester.

Printed in the United States of America

ISBN: 0936073-08-X

Foreword

According to the most reliable estimates, over 13 million Americans observed Kwanzaa (December 26th-January 1st). Yet in spite of these impressive numbers, confusion still surrounds this most unusual holiday. The confusion primarily stems from the true nature of the holiday's origin.

Since its inception in 1966, myths and misconceptions have been symbiotic by-products. Many assume that Kwanzaa is a transported Christmas substitute. Perhaps this belief stems from the fact that Kwanzaa begins the day after Christmas. Kwanzaa could best be described as a cultural reaffirmation. A time for African-Americans to reflect upon their rich cultural heritage, as products of two worlds.

Kwanzaa: Everything You Always Wanted To Know, But Didn't Know Where to Ask, is the definitive book on Kwanzaa; its origins, principles and practice. This book offers inexpensive celebration ideas, recipes, fashions, and home decorating tips. It serves as a comprehensive guide for the scholar, celebrant, and anyone interested in contemporary American culture.

Kwanzaa: Everything You Always Wanted To Know, But Didn't Know Where To Ask, will become a modern classic, and a staple in every home.

DEDICATION

To Those Who Have Made The Final Transition

To my great-grandmother, Nanny B. Smith who helped nurture me and made me feel special because of her unconditional love. To my grandmother, Madeline Boyd who taught me what a wonderful gift an active imagination could be by the nightly stories she would concoct to get me to go to sleep. To my great-aunt Mabel Coles who we affectionately called "Arnie" for teaching me that the finer things in life are attainable. To my Aunt Mary Newman who showed me the meaning of love. To my uncle Billy Boyd for teaching me to view death as a transition. To my step-father, Henry Rogers, color him father, color him love. To all of the ancestors who have preceded me on both shores, Though you are gone you will never be forgotten for your collective spirits flow through me.

To The Living

To my mother who instilled in me a belief that all things are possible with faith. Thank you for all that you have given in the past, and for all that you continue to give.To my favorite Aunt Mabel. To my brother Mike, continue to keep your head to the sky, I have more faith in you than you realize. To Kenny B., through thick and thin you knew me when. To my children Mashairi and Ho-Toi who bring me untold joy and extra grey hairs. To Cynthia and Speedy for similar reasons. To my main man Leroy, remember your not afraid of a man or giant. That's why they call you Leroy Bryant. To uncle Cecil for your positive influence and your fine sense of humor. To my cousins Brad and Donna and Cecil, Stevie, and Bruce, I love you all. To Boston and all of my childhood memories. To New York my second home. To all who have wished me well and to those who haven't. Thanks Vivian for your invaluable assistance. Thanks Dumar for your occasional spirts of inspiration (smile). A special thanks to Mr. Jose Ferrer a true marketing genius and a living example of the Kwanzaa principles. To Mr. Joseph Kelly and the rest of the C.A.S.H. team. A very special thanks to Cookie who has made my life richer. To all others, Allah is still one God.

About the Author

Cedric McClester is a syndicated columnist and journalist. His thought provoking news articles and commentaries have appeared in both national and international publications. Mr. McClester received his undergraduate degree from The College for Human Services where he graduated with honors. He also holds a Masters degree in Education from Fordham University.

Mr. McClester has been affiliated with the New York Urban Coalition, sponsors of the nation's largest public Kwanzaa celebrations. As a result of its efforts, Kwanzaa has become institutionalized to the point where annual celebrations are co-hosted by The American Museum of Natural History in New York City.

Mr. McClester, former editor-in-chief of *Kwanzaa* magazine, published by The New York Urban Coalition states, "The true significance of Kwanzaa lies in the seven principles it is based on. Unity, self-determination, collective work and responsibility, cooperative economics, purpose, creativity, and faith are not only good principles to live by, they are also universally recognized as proper guides for cohesive socialization."

Bronze panels from Benin, Nigeria

Contents

The Libation Statement

It is tradition to pour libation in remembrance of the ancestors on all special occasions. Kwanzaa, is such an occasion, as it provides us with an opportunity to reflect upon our African past and American present. Water is suggested as it holds the essence of life. Libation should be placed in a communal cup and poured in the direction of the four winds i.e. north, south, east, and west. It should then be passed among family members and guests who may either sip from the cup or make a sipping gesture.

For The Motherland cradle of civilization.
For the ancestors and their indomitable spirit.
For the elders from whom we can learn much.
For our youth who represent the promise for tomorrow.
For our people the original people.
For our struggle and in remembrance of those who have struggled on our behalf.
For Umoja the priniciple of unity which should guide us in all that we do.
For the creator who provides all things great and small.

Preface

It is no more than fitting that proper homage be paid to Dr. Maulana "Ron" Karenga who founded Kwanzaa in 1966. During the 1960's, Dr. Karenga was a leading theorist of The Black Movement. He has authored numerous scholarly articles on various aspects of Black life and struggle which have appeared in major anthologies and journals. What he began as a cultural idea and an expression of the Us organization which he headed, has blossomed into the only nationally celebrated, indigenous, non-religious, non-heroic, non-political African-American holiday.

As African-Americans abandoned their negative self-images and started adapting natural hairstyles and traditional dress, the desire for ties to their African past increased. Kwanzaa became the ideal forum for exploring these cultural roots, while recognizing the unique heritage of African-Americans as products of both worlds. In the haste to address the demand for all things of a cultural nature, information concerning the concept, origin and practice of Kwanzaa has been incomplete. This has been the result of inadequate research in some instances and a refusal on the part of some to believe that an American Black man could conceive and perpetuate a holiday of Kwanzaa's magnitude.

Kwanzaa: Everything You Always Wanted To Know But Didn't Know Where to Ask, explains the origin, concepts, and practice of Kwanzaa in a clear concise manner, and offers recipes, fashion ideas, celebration suggestions and hairstyles, along with a suggested reading list. This book will become an indispensible guide for those desiring to celebrate Kwanzaa, the newest edition to the December holidays.

Family Gathering—Pen and ink
Dindga McCannon (Courtesy Grinnell Gallery)

Most Commonly Asked Questions About Kwanzaa

Question: *What is Kwanzaa?*
Answer: Kwanzaa is a unique American Holiday that pays tribute to the rich cultural roots of Americans of African ancestry.

Q. *What is the meaning of the word Kwanzaa?*
A. Kwanzaa means "the first" or "the first fruits of the harvest", in the East African language of Kiswahili.

Q. *When is Kwanzaa observed?*
A. Kwanzaa is observed from December 26th through January 1st.

Q. *What is the origin of Kwanzaa?*
A. Kwanzaa was founded in 1966 by Dr. Maulana Karenga, a Black Studies professor who describes himself as a cultural nationalist. Kwanzaa originated as a cultural idea and an expression of the nationalist Us organization which was headed by Dr. Karenga.

Q. *Is Kwanzaa a religious holiday?*
A. Kwanzaa is unique in that it is neither a religious, political, nor heroic but rather a cultural one.

Q. *What is Kwanzaa based on?*
A. Kwanzaa is based on seven fundamental principles which are referred to as the **Nguzo Saba.**

Q. *What are those principles?*
A. Unity, **Umoja** (U-mo-ja); Self-determination, **Kujichagulia** (Ku-ji-cha-gu-

1

lia); Collective work and responsibility, **Ujima** (U-ji-ma); Cooperative economics, **Ujamaa** (U-ja-ma); Purpose, **Nia;** Creativity, **Kuumba** (Ku-um-ba); and faith, **Imani** (I-mani).

Q. *Is Kwanzaa a Christmas substitute?*
A. No, though Dr. Karenga recognized the undue hardship that the over commercialization of Christmas has for Black people and others who are at the lowest rung of the social strata. Therefore, those who find Kwanzaa to be more meaningful to them, now have an option and can still be part of the holiday season.

Q. *How important is gift giving during Kwanzaa?*
A. Gifts may be exchanged during Kwanzaa though it is suggested that they not be given if they present undue hardship. When gifts are given it is suggested that they be creative i.e. handmade or functional like a book.

Q. *How is Kwanzaa Celebrated?*
A. Kwanzaa can be celebrated in a number of ways. At a bare minimum a table should be prepared with the following items: A place mat **(Mkeka)** usually made of straw; a candle holder for seven candles **(Kinara);** seven candles **(Mishumaa saba);** a variety of fruit **(Mazao)** ears of corn **(Vibunzi)** representing the number of children in the home; gifts if any **(Zawadi);** and a unity or communal cup **(Kikombe cha umoja)** for pouring and sharing libation. Each day of Kwanzaa a candle should be lit beginning with the black candle which is placed in the center of the candle holder. Candles are then lit alternately from left to right. Three green candles should be placed on the left and three red candles should be placed on the right. Each day a principle should be recited when the candle was lit. The importance that each principle has for the person reciting it should be expounded upon. Other suggestions can be found in this book.

Q. *Why is kiswahili used?*
A. Kiswahili was chosen because it is a non-tribal African language that encompasses a large portion of the African continent. An added benefit is that Swahili pronounciation is extremely easy. Vowels are pronounced like those in Spanish and the consonants with few exceptions like those of English. The vowels are as follows: **A=ah** as in **father; E=a** as in **day; I=ee** as in **free; O=oo** as in **too.** The accent is almost always on the next to the last syllable.

Nguzo Saba (The Seven Principles)

Listed below are The Seven Principles of Kwanzaa, which may serve as guides for daily living.

1. Umoja (Unity)
To strive for and maintain unity in the family, community, nation and race.

2. Kujichagulia (Self-determination)
To define ourselves, name ourselves, create for ourselves and speak for ourselves instead of being defined, named, created for and spoken for by others.

3. Ujima (Collective Work and Responsibility)
To build and maintain our community together and make our sister's and brother's problems our problems and to solve them together.

4. Ujamaa (Cooperative Economics)
To build and maintain our own stores, shops and other businesses and to profit from them together.

5. Nia (Purpose)
To make our collective vocation the building and developing our community in order to restore our people to their traditional greatness.

6. Kuumba (Creativity)
To do always as much as we can, in the way we can, in order to leave our community more beautiful and beneficial than we inherited it.

7. Imani (Faith)

To believe with all our heart in our people, our parents, our teachers, our leaders and the righteousness and victory of our struggle.

Dr. Maulana Karenga
7 September, 1965

Kwanzaa—Pen and ink
Charlotte Richardson (Courtesy Grinnell Gallery)

Kwanzaa Symbols

Like other holidays Kwanzaa has its symbols. These symbols are instructive and inspirational objects that represent and reinforce desirable principles, concepts and practices. There are seven basic symbols and two optional symbols that are both traditional and modern items and therefore reflect traditional, as well as modern concepts which evolved out of the life and struggle of African-American people.

The seven basic symbols of Kwanzaa are:

1. **Mazao** (fruit and vegetables)
2. **Mkeka** (place mat)
3. **Kinara** (the candle holder for seven candles one black, three red, and three green)
4. **Vibunzi** (ears of corn reflective of the number of children in the home)
5. **Zawadi** (gifts)
6. **Kikombe Cha Umoja** (communal unity cup)
7. **Mishumaa Saba** (the seven candles)

The two optional, or supplementary symbols are the **Nguzo Saba** (seven principles) usually printed in large letters for all to see and the **Bendera ya Taifa** (The national flag or standard). The bendera is the black, red, and green flag given to us by the father of the modern Black nationalist movement, Marcus Garvey. Red was for the blood our people shed. Green was for hope and is the color of the Motherland, and black was for the face of our people.

5

Dr. Karenga explains, "In the 60's we reordered the colors and slightly adjusted their interpretation to correspond to our current needs." *(Kwanzaa: Origin, Concepts, Practice,* by Maulana Karenga, p. 23). Therefore, black is mentioned first because the people came first. Red is mentioned next not simply for the blood that was shed, but also as a symbol of our continuing struggle. Finally green represents our bountiful motherland, Africa as well as the hopes and aspirations for the future our youths represent.

1. *Mazao* (Crops i.e. fruits and vegetables)

The mazao have significance because they symbolize the rewards of collective productive labor. Moreover, as Kwanzaa means first or first fruits and it was patterned after the traditional celebrations that take place among African agricultural societies at harvest time. At harvest time the fruits of collective labor abound and it is a time of great joy and togetherness, a time for Thanksgiving and remembrance. The mazao therefore, represent the historical roots of the holiday itself.

2. *Mkeka* (Place mat)

Dr. Karenga states, "The **mkeka** is the symbol of tradition and by extension history." He adds, "Since Kwanzaa seeks to inspire appreciation and practice of values which aid us in our lives and struggle, the stress on tradition and history become unavoidable." One can not escape tradition and history, for they form the foundation on which correct knowledge and true understanding are built. The ancestors understood this clearly, as illustrated by the following proverb: "If you know the beginning well, the end will not trouble you."

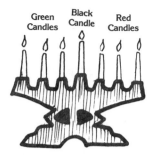

Green Candles Black Candle Red Candles

3. *Kinara* (Candleholder)

The kinara is symbolic of the continental Africans, our parent people. In incorporating this symbol, Dr. Karenga used a Zulu concept. In early Kwanzaa celebrations, the kinara was used to symbolize Nkulunkulu, the first born, the father of both our people and our principles. Since the early days of Kwanzaa, the kinara has come to symbolize our ancestors as a collective whole.

4. *Vibunzi* (Ears of corn)

The Vibunzi represent children thus, each family uses as many ears of corn as it has children. Karenga states, "In traditional terminology, the ears of corn represent the produce of the stalk, and the potential, of the offspring to become stalks or producers and reproducers themselves, thus insuring the immortality of the people or nation." Emphasis is placed on children, for they truly represent the hope for the future. Therefore, if we instill the proper values in them and teach them the benefits of mutual respect, we insure a brighter tomorrow when we become elders.

5. *Zawadi* (Gifts)

Zawadi should be given as a reward for commitments made and kept and are usually exchanged among members of a nuclear family. They should be given to reinforce personal growth and achievement which benefits the collective. Gifts given during Kwanzaa are not given automatically, but are rather based on merit. They should be of an educational or otherwise beneficial nature. Books make excellent gifts. Those things that are handmade are encouraged. One should not fall victim to the commercialism that presently characterizes Christmas.

6. *Kikombe Cha Umoja* (The communal unity cup)

Clearly, as the name suggests, the unity cup symbolizes the first and most important principle of Kwanzaa, unity. It is used to pour Tambiko (libation) in the direction of the four winds, north, south, east, and west, in rememberance of the ancestors. The unity cup may then be passed among members of the family and guests who may either choose to sip or make a sipping gesture. This is done to honor the ancestors and to promote the spirit of oneness.

7. *Mishumaa Saba* (The seven candles)

The Mishumaa Saba represent the **Nguzo Saba** (The seven principles) which are at the heart of the value system that is the foundation of Kwanzaa. According to Dr. Karenga, "**The Nguzo Saba** have their roots in research of African cultures which revealed recurrent value emphasis, values that reinforced the bonds between the people and increased their human possibilities for meaningful and fulfilling life". As each candle represents a distinct principle beginning with Umoja (unity, the black center candle), and candle is lit each day from left to right after the Umoja candle has been lit.

The Kwanzaa Karamu (feast)

The evening of December 31st has special significance because the Kwanzaa Karamu is held then. The karamu allows for cultural expression, as well as for feasting. There should be a wide variety of various foods as all attending should take responsibility for preparing a dish, or several dishes. Single persons may bring a dish or they may elect to bring fruit, bread or anything else that might enhance the meal.

It is important to decorate the place where the karamu will be held, (e.g. home, community center, church) in an African motif that utilizes a black, red, and green color scheme. A large Kwanzaa setting should dominate the room where the karamu will take place. A large **Mkeka** should be placed in the center of the floor where the food should be placed creatively and made accessible to all for self-service. Prior to and during the feast, an informative and entertaining program should be presented. Traditionally, the program involves welcoming, remembering, reassessment, recommitment and rejoicing, concluded by a farewell statement and call for greater unity.

Below is a suggested format for the Karamu program, from a model by Dr. Karenga.

Kukaribisha (Welcoming)
Introductory Remarks and Recognition of Distinguished Guests and All Elders.
Cultural Expression*

*Songs, music, group dancing, poetry, performances, chants, unity circles, etc.

9

Kukumbuka (remembering)
Reflections of a Man, Woman and Child.
Cultural Expression.

Kuchunguza Tena Na Kutoa Ahadi Tena
(Reassessment and Recommitment)
Introduction of Distinguished Guest Lecturer and Short
Talk.

Kushangilia (Rejoicing)
Tamshi la Tambiko (Libation Statement)**
Kikombe cha Umoja (Unity Cup)
Kutoa Majina (Calling Names of Family Ancestors and
Black Heroes)
Ngoma (Drums)
Karamu (Feast)
Cultural Expression

Tamshi la Tutaonana (The Farewell Statement)

**See page ix of this book.

Kwanzaa Menu Suggestions

As with other traditional holidays that have established meals, Kwanzaa too has a traditional menu. This menu was put together based on the seven principles, especially **Ujima, Ujamaa** and **Kuumba.** Collectively we come together to provide an economical meal. All it takes is inspiration and creativity to put together a celebration that will be remembered throughout the years.

During Kwanzaa we fast from sunrise to sunset to cleanse our bodies, minds and spirits. During the evening meal when we break our daily fast we light the appropriate candle which coincides with the principle of that day. The spirit of Kwanzaa teaches us to share our home, food and drink and music as our ancestors did during the hunt or harvest. We must do the same today and invite other family members, friends and neighbors to our home to rejoice collectively in a meaningful way to strengthen unity. Harambee! (let's pull together).[1]

[1]By Joanne Baylor. Reprinted by permission from *Kwanzaa* magazine, published by The New York Urban Coalition.

Kwanzaa Fried Chicken
by Nancy Moore

1 whole fryer cut into parts
¼ cup of hot sauce
1 tablespoon of mustard
1 cup of flour
1 tablespoon of cornmeal
¼ cup Italian bread crumbs
2 tablespoons of Bisquick
1 teaspoon of baking powder

Pour hot sauce and mustard in bowl. Rub chicken throughly in bowl and let stand for 10 minutes. Place flour, cornmeal, bread crumbs, bisquick, baking powder in plastic bag. Salt and pepper to taste. Drop chicken in bag and shake well. Preheat iron skillet. Pour ½ pan of oil until hot, drop chicken in oil. Do not crowd. Cook on high flame until light brown on one side. Lower flame and cover until almost crispy brown. Remove cover and let cook 3 more minutes before turning over and turning gas back up. Cook until crispy brown. Drain and lay on hand towels. Serves 4 people.

Baked Bluefish Supreme
By Nancy Moore

4 lbs of bluefish
Two onions thin sliced
Pinch of garlic powder
Two tablespoons of papricka
Pinch of oregano
Pinch of ginger
Onion bits
1 green pepper thin sliced
Two tablespoons Italian bread crumbs

Oil bottom of pan well. Pre-heat oven to 350°. Lay fish in pan after placing onions and green peppers. Then place ingredients on top of fish seal tight with tinfoil. Cook approximately 10 to 15 minutes. Serves 8 people.

Simply Heavenly Baked Fish
By Pat Davis

2 lbs. filet fish
1 cup mayonnaise
1 cup sour cream
½ lb. green seedless grapes

Mix mayonnaise and sour cream, then place one layer of fish on the bottom of baking dish. Next place the mayo mixture on top, then the grapes. Keep repeating this process until all the fish is used up. You should end up with the green grapes on top. Bake for 20 minutes. Serves 4 people. Enjoy.

Nice Rice
by Nancy Moore

1 cup of long stem rice
1 tablespoon of butter or margarine
½ teaspoon of curry
⅓ cup of water or chicken broth

Place butter in pan. Add rice and water under high flame. Bring to rapid boil. Cover tightly and turn flame as low as possible. Cook approximately a ½ hour. Serves 4 people.

Dandy Candied Yams
By Nancy Moore

1 large can of yams
1 fresh lemon
1 fresh orange
¼ lbs. of butter
½ cup of brown sugar

½ teaspoon of mace
½ teaspoon of allspice
2 tablespoons of pureed coconut
1 dash of salt

Place butter in saucepan under low flame. Add ¼ teaspoon of lemon and ¼ teaspoon of orange juice. Add other ingredients and stir well until smooth consistency. Slice yams and place in baking pan. Pour mixture over yams and let sit for 3 minutes. Place yams in preheated oven (350°) until bubbling brown on top. Approximately 15-20 minutes. Serves 5 people.

Rice Cheese Balls
by Ayesha Jihada

2 cups of brown rice
4 cups grated sharp cheese
4 eggs well beaten
4 cups Italian flavored bread
crumbs
Vegetable oil
Vegetable salt

Cook rice in a 8 qt. pot, using instructions for firm rice on the package. While rice is cooking, grate cheese into rice immediately after cooking, while rice is still hot. Form balls while mixture is hot and sticky. If mixture cools off before you finish, warm it on a low flame. Dip balls into eggs first, then coat with bread crumbs. Pre-heat vegetable oil in large frying pan until it sizzles when a drop of water is carefully flicked in. Fry cheese balls until they are golden brown on all sides, and crispy.

Note: Rice cheese balls are a favorite in our house. The children love to participate in the cooking part as well as in the eating part. Forming and shaping the balls provides practice of manipulative skills for the 4-year old, and dipping in eggs and bread crumbs allows you to feel different textures, get messy, learn about wet and dry, and participate in a grown-up activity. I also use cooking activity time to discuss nutrition and the value of cooperation: "Two can get it done faster than one." This recipe is high in protein, and heavy, so a nice tossed salad goes well with it.

Sweet Potato Pie
by Pam Douglas

4 medium yams
1 cup sugar
½ stick of butter
¼ tsp. salt
½ cup coconut
1 tbsp. nutmeg or cinnamon

1 tbsp. of flavor
¼ tsp. vanilla
3 eggs, separated
⅓ cup milk
1 unbaked 9" pie crust

Boil yams - well done. Peel and mash. Mix in large bowl yams, sugar, butter and salt. Beat well. Add milk, lemon flavor, coconut, nutmeg and egg yolks. Continue beating. Beat egg whites until fluffy. Fold into mixture. Pour into pie crust shell (1 - 9" deep pie plate). Bake in 350° oven 35-45 minutes.

African Togetherness Health Salad
by Black Rose

Cracked *wheat*
Grated *carrots*
Grated *beets*
Chopped *scallions*
Tofu
Raisins
Sunflower seeds
Broccoli
Spinach *or any green vegetable*

Combine; Loving herbal seasonings:
thyme
basil
sage
ginger
fresh or grounded cayanne pepper
parsely

Use mayonnaise that contains no sugar, salt, or eggs or tamari, tahini sauce. Combine seasonings stated above, stir & mix. Portions make plenty of everything, and mix with your own vibrations.

Note: adjust amounts of ingredients according to your taste, and amount of servings.

Do Do (Plantain)
by Black Rose

Nigerians call plantain "Do Do" (pronounced "dough, dough"). This recipe is Do Do with a contemporary African vibe. Slice thickly, a very ripe plantain and base lightly with palm oil. Sprinkle with cayenne pepper and nutmeg. Wrap in tinfoil and broil.

African Lady—Woodcut print
James Sepyo (Courtesy Grinnell Gallery)

Afrocentric Hairstyles

In keeping with the spirit of Kwanzaa, many Black women wear their hair in one of the many beautiful African-inspired styles.

The Art of Cornrowing

The ancient art of cornrowing is one that has been handed down through the generations in African Womens' beauty habits, but it is also an expression of communion with the universe.

It has been said that cornrowing is a basic aesthetic of the African woman's existence. Millions of women from West, South, East, and Central Africa consider cornrowing a living art form. The variations are infinite and no one style appears the same way on any one woman. Nigeria, where cornrowing is looked upon as an art akin to spirituality and ritual is an example of this. Traditionally, among the Yoruba, the most decorative and intricate styles were worn by priestesses and queens. Cornrowing not only symbolized status, but was also a sign of age. Simple, basic styles were worn by young girls and older women, while the more elaborate styles were worn by marriagable women.

Cornrowing provides today's Black woman with an aesthetically pleasing way of reflecting pride in who they are, where they came from and their rich cultural heritage.

Start with the Basics - Step 1

To begin oil and brush your hair. Then part the hair into 3 sections, as if you were

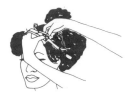

going to braid a pigtail. Hold only a minimum amount of hair at a time and begin to interweave sections. Interweave section 3 over section 2. Then part the lower portion of 3.

Moving Right Along - Step 2

This should be done similtaneously while plucking hair from the roots and weaving it into each section. all cornrowing should be done flat on the surface of the scalp. When you reach the end of the hair, simply twist or braid the hair.

Join sections 3 and 4 under section 1. Section 1 should be in the middle over sections 3 and 4.

I Think You've Got It - Step 3

Maintaining harmony with the parted scalp is essential to the success of any cornrow style. Cornrows should be tight, so the tighter, the better. Thickness depends upon your own individual hair, as does the amount of time involved. It is possible to spend 45 minutes or 3 hours or more cornrowing.

Join section 5 with section 2. Twist section 2, 3, and 4 around section 1. Section 1 should join section 6. All sections should now be interwoven.

Now that you have finished cornrowing, you are ready to begin experimenting with the countless hairstyles available to beautiful Black women.

How to Add Extensions

If you have short or thin hair and would like to wear one of the longer braided styles, this may be achieved by adding synthetic or human hair pieces (extensions). To begin, detach several small sections from your hairpiece and lay them close by.

Shall We Begin? Step 1

Evenly part a section of your own hair and either at the beginning of your braid or midway into the braid, lay the extension over the natural hair. The center of the extension should meet the natural hair section.

Got the Idea? Step 2

Start to braid, passing section a under section c and over section b.

Keep on Keeping On - Step 3

Pass section b over section c. The extension should now be securely in place.

Wow! You've Got It Now - Step 4

Pull some hair form section b forming section d and blend into natural hair (section c). Then complete your braid.

19

Hair Grooming Hints

Care of the Cornrow
When cornrowing, the hair should be wet, already conditioned and toweled. Comb and brush the hair throughly and then add oil or conditioner. Then begin parting and cornrowing. Depending upon the wetness of the hair, a few minutes under the dryer might be advisable.

Care of The Scalp
Cornrowing can be quite healthy for the scalp. Be sure you oil your scalp and hair daily while in cornrows. Actually, the cornrows will remain in place longer if they are oiled daily and if at night the hair is tied or capped before going to sleep.

A Word About Cornrowing and Plaiting
Cornrowing is an underhand motion while plaiting is another name for traditional braiding or pigtailing. French rolling, which is necessary for styling combinations, is merely cornrowing in reverse in an overhand motion.

Sewing Beads Into Hair
For sewing you will need thick thread (The same color as the hair). Knot the thread at the end and sew it into hair, hiding the knot. Place small beads onto the thread, pushing them all the way down to the end. Now sew again. The entire pattern is then a "space and sew, space and sew" routine. Do not go all the way to the scalp in sewing, only on top of the cornrow. Repeat this pattern until hair is adorned to your satisfaction.

Beading the Hair
Adorning the hair with beads is easy and adds color and flair to almost any natural or cornrowed style. All you need are small hairpins, bobby pins and, of course beads. Just place the hairpin through the hole in the beads. Then slowly stick the beaded hairpin into the hair. Let go of the grip, pushing the hairpin into the hair. Now that the beading is done; make any design you choose. Note: beads can be taken out as easily as put in. It is suggested that they be removed before going to bed at night.

Putting Shells into Hair
Shells add a sense of glamor and zest to even the most modest hair style. Shells can be strung on string or thread. Once the shells are on string or thread, attach them to the hair. Shells can be wrapped into braids or cornrows. Wrap then as if the string or thread were part of the hair. The same procedure can be followed for adorning the hair with bells or rubber bands.

Hairstyles by Donna Moses

Reprinted by permission from *Accent African: Traditional and Contemporary Hairstyles for the Black Woman* · 2nd edition by Valarie Thomas · Osborne, © 1982. Published by Col · Bob Associates, Inc. New York.

Samples of West African textiles (Top) Okene silk cloth, *Nigeria;* (Top Center) Ashante Kente cloth strip, *Ghana;* (Left) Ibo woman's cloth, *Nigeria;* (Center) woman's cloth, *Nigeria;* (Right) Yoruba woman's cloth, *Nigeria.*

Kwanzaa Fashion Suggestions

When deciding upon what to wear during Kwanzaa, a couple of things should be kept in mind. First and foremost, Kwanzaa is a cultural holiday, a time for African-Americans to pay tribute to their richly diverse cultural heritage. As products of both Africa and America, the cultural imprints of both influences should be displayed. Therefore, western dress may be accentuated with African fabrics. In African dress, color plays an important part as you shall see later. Color is also important in Kwanzaa. Black, red, and green are the symbolic colors, and this should be kept in mind when choosing clothes to wear.

Second, **Kuumba** (Creativity) is the sixth principle of Kwanzaa, and should be employed whenever possible. As an innately creative people, we are called upon during Kwanzaa, and throughout the year to let our creative juices flow. An abundance of creativity can be seen in African textiles. At this juncture it would be helpful to provide you with a working knowledge of the cultural context of these textiles.

The Cultural Context of Textiles

The most obvious use of textiles are as articles of clothing. One or more lengths of cloth may be draped around the body, or tailored to make gowns, tunics, and pants. Protection against the elements and making our bodies more attractive, are not the only purpose of clothing. As started earlier, color plays an important role in African dress. Particular colors or decorative embellishments or shapes of garments may have a prestige value; that the wearer is immediately marked as having great wealth or status.

Certain colors decorations or shapes of garments may also have significance in a political or ritual context. The tribal affiliations of a Moroccan Berber woman for example, can be read in the pattern of stripes on her cloak. In Benin, Nigeria, chiefs wear red cloth as part of their cermonial court dress, and the color by its association with anger, blood, war, and fire is regarded as threatening. By wearing such cloth, it is thought that a chief protects himself, and his king from evil.

The basic color spectrum of Africa; red, black, and white is rarely without some level of meaning. Similarly the colors of Kwanzaa; black, red, and green have significance as explained earlier. In some parts of Nigeria, among the Igbirra for example, red is a color associated with success and achievement.

The Art of Headwrapping

One of the easiest Afrocentric items that can be worn during Kwanzaa is the Gele. Below are instructions and illustrations on the art of headwrapping.

Step 1
Use a two yard length of fabric 45" wide. The two raw ends of the gele can be folded and machine hemmed if desired. Fold the length of the Gele as indicated.

Step 2
Begin the wrap on the left side of your head, with the short ends facing the back of the head.

24

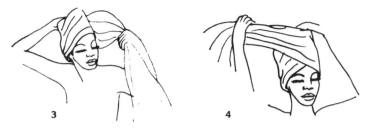

Step 3
While holding the beginning portion securely, wrap the length around (low on the forehead) and toward the back. Continue wrapping around the back and up the left side, overlapping where you began.

Step 4
As you approach the center front of the forehead, it should form an inverted V.

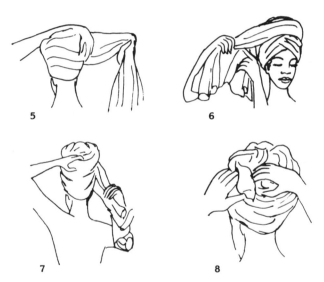

Step 5, 6, 7
Continue to wrap as illustrated in steps 5, 6, 7.

Step 8
The tail of the wrap should be brought around the side or back of the head and tucked securely between the folds.

Reprinted by permission from *Accent African Fashions* © 1975. Published by Col-Bob Associates, Inc.

Breaking Bread—Pen and ink
Ademola Olugebefola (Courtesy Grinnell Gallery)

Celebrating Kwanzaa

As it is always better to get an early start, I suggest that you begin the first week in December by making a check list. On your list you should check for the following items: A **Kinara** (candle holder); **Mkeka** (place mat preferrably made of straw); **Mazao** (crops i.e. fruits and vegetables); **Vibunzi** (ears of corn to reflect the number of children in the household); **Kikombe cha umoja** (communal unity cup); **Mishumaa saba** (seven candles, one black, three red, and three green); and **Zwaidi** (gifts that are enriching).

It is important that the **Kinara** not be confused with the minorah. The **Kinara** holds seven candles to reflect the seven principles which are the foundation of Kwanzaa, while the minorah is a Jewish religious symbol that holds eight candles. If you don't have a **Kinara** and don't know where to get one, it is suggested that you use "kuumba" (creativity) and make one. A two by four or a piece of driftwood will do just fine, and screw-in candle holders can be purchased in most hardware stores. The **Mkeka** (place mat) shouldn't present a problem. While straw is suggested because it is traditional, cloth makes an adequate substitute. If cloth is used, one with an African print is preferred. The other symbols are easy to come by and warrant no further discussion other than to caution against placing the **Mazao** (crops) in a cornucopia which is Western. A plain straw basket or a bowl will do just fine.

One last note, even households with no children should place an ear of corn on the place mat to symbolize the African concept of social parenthood. All seven symbols are creatively placed on top of the place mat i.e. The symbols should be attractively arranged as they form the Kwanzaa centerpiece.

Gifts

Kuumba (creativity) is greatly encouraged. Not only is **Kuumba** one of the seven principles, it also brings a sense of personal satisfaction and puts one squarely into the spirit of Kwanzaa. Therefore, those symbols that can be made, should be made. *To buy everything ready made is to burden Kwanzaa with the kind of commercialism that presently plagues Christmas. The giving of gifts during Kwanzaa does not contradict this, as gifts should be affordable and of an educational or artistic nature.* Gifts are usually exchanged between parents and children and traditionally given on January 1st the last day of Kwanzaa. However gift giving during Kwanzaa may occur at any time.

Decorating the Home

The **Kinara** along with the other symbols of Kwanzaa should dominate the room, which should be given an African motif. This is easily achieved and shouldn't result in too much expense. As the colors of Kwanzaa are black, red, and green. This should be kept in mind when decorating the home. Black, red, and green streamers, balloons, cloth, flowers, and African prints can be hung tastefully around the room. Original art and sculpture may be displayed as well.

The Kwanzaa Feast or Karamu

The Kwanzaa Karamu* is traditionally held on December 31st, (participants celebrating New Year's Eve, should plan their Karamu early in the evening). It is a very special event as it is the one Kwanzaa event that brings us closer to our African roots. The Karamu is a communal and cooperative effort. Ceremonies and cultural expressions are highly encouraged.

*See page 9 of this book.

Musician—Pen and ink
Abdullah Aziz (Courtesy Grinnell Gallery)

Journey To See The Butterfly—Woodcut print
James Sepyo (Courtesy Grinnell Gallery)

Zawadi (Gifts)

As stated earlier **Kuumba** (creativity) is highly encouraged during Kwanzaa. However it is recognized that in today's hectic world, we do not always have the time to create the gifts we wish to give, not to mention that everyone is not creatively inclined. Gifts should be based on merit and a concerted effort made to patronize our community merchants, one of the principles of Kwanzaa **Ujamaa** (Cooperative Economics).

When purchasing gifts for Kwanzaa, keep in mind that they should be of an educational, creative, or inspirational in nature and not cause undue economic hardship on the buyer.

Listed below are suggested gifts for Kwanzaa.

- Books written by and about Africans and African-Americans and the diaspora
- Art prints
- Original paintings and sculpture by African and African-American artists
- Tickets to cultural events
- Educational games and/or toys
- Hand made toys/clothes/accessories
- Handicrafts
- Ethnic dolls
- African, Caribbean, Central and South American imports (leather, weavings, clothing).

Visions II—Carbon pencil
Abdul Rahman (Courtesy Grinnell Gallery)

Kwanzaa Gift Shopper's Guide

In the spirit of **Ujamaa** (Cooperative Economics), the Publishers have included a selected list of stores in the United States, selling Kwanzaa books, greeting cards and other cultural items.

SELECTED LISTING

ALABAMA

Personal Treasures
Attn: Gloria Young Logan
2209 Marshall Ave. N.W.
Huntsville, AL 35810
(205) 852-7902
Children and adult books, gifts & related crafts reflecting the African-American experience.

CALIFORNIA

University of Sankore Press
2560 West 54th Street
Los Angeles, CA 90043
(213) 295-9799
Publishers of "The African-American Holiday of Kwanzaa: A Celebration of Family, Community & Culture" by Dr. Maulana Karenga, the creator of Kwanzaa.

Culture Collection
Attn: Betty Davis
1010 B. Florin Road #225
Sacramento, CA 95831
(916) 393-1718
Books, artifacts, cards and items related to the black positive experience.

The Black Earth
Attn: Beverly Hicks
450 Santa Clara Avenue
Oakland, CA 94610
(415) 465-4145
Variety of books, greeting cards and merchandise highlighting afrocentricity.

33

FLORIDA

Afro In Books-N-Things
Attn: Mary Wells
5575 N.W. 7th Avenue
Miami, FL 33127
(305) 756-6107
Books reflecting the black experience, greeting cards and other culturally related items.

GEORGIA

Shrine of the Black Madonna Bookstore
Attn: Velma Thomas
946 Abernathy Blvd. S.W.
Atlanta, GA 30310
(404) 752-6125
A vast selection of books, cards, posters & items reflecting Africentric creativity.

KENTUCKY

Aikebu-Lan Images
2600 W. Broadway
Louisville, KY 40211
(502) 778-9633
Afro-American art, artifacts, books, positive apparel, books and Kwanzaa celebration sets.

MASSACHUSETTS

Savanna Books
Attn: Gail P. Willet
858 Massachusetts Avenue
Cambridge, MA 02139
(617) 868-3423
Specializing in books about children of color.

MICHIGAN

Shrine of the Black Madonna Bookstore
Attn: Ayele or Barbara Martin
13534 Livernois Avenue
Detroit, MI 48238
(313) 491-0777
A vast selection of books, cards, posters, gifts & items reflecting africentric creativity.

The Robinson Collection
Attn: Robyn Robinson
527 E. Michigan Avenue
Kalamazoo, MI 49007
A selection of fine books, gifts, collectibles, fine art prints, dolls and cards.

MISSOURI

First World Collection
St. Louis Union Station
1820 Market Street
St. Louis, MO 63104
(314) 421-3433
Africentric gifts, attire, books, imports, jewelry and arts.

NEW JERSEY

Tunde Dada - House of Africa
Attn: Temi
347 Main Street
Orange, NJ 07050
(201) 673-4446
Afro-centric books, gifts, art & clothes.

NEW YORK

Lushena Books
Attn: Luther Warner
15 West 24th Street
New York, NY 10010
(212) 989-0080
Distributor of afro-centric books, dolls, calendars and greeting cards.

NORTH CAROLINA

Special Occasions
112 M.L.K. Jr. Drive
Winston-Salem, NC 27101
(919) 724-0334 or (1-800) 321-3046
A fine selection of books, art, cards, greek paraphernalia & church supplies.

OHIO

Shadow Box People
Attn: Debra Newton
680 Malvern Avenue
Columbus, OH 43219
(614) 258-7103
Dolls, books, puzzles & posters.

34

Artistic Apparel
7030 Reading Road
Swifton Commons Mall
Cincinnati, OH 45237
(513) 351-ARTS (2787)
African-American art, artifacts, books, positive apparel and custom silk screening.

TENNESSEE
Alkebu-Lan Images, Inc.
Attn: Yusef
2721 Jefferson Street
Nashville, TN 37208
(615) 321-4111
Afro-American art, artifacts, books, positive apparel & Kwanzaa celebrations sets.

TEXAS
African-American Reflections
Attn: Sheila Drennan
Windsor Park Mall
7900 I.H. 35 North
San Antonio, TX 78218
(512) 657-2376
Books, antiques, fabric posters and other items pertaining to Black history and culture.

Amistad Bookplace
Attn: Denise Armstrong
1413 Holman Street
Houston, TX 77004
(713) 528-3561
Specializing in Afro-American culture books, cards, posters and related items.

Amistad II - University Bookstore
Attn: Ms. E. Carreathers
705 University Drive
Prairie View, TX 77446
(409) 857-9101
Specializing in Afro-American culture books, cards, posters and related items.

Pan African Connection Bookstore
Attn: Akwehe
300 S. Beckley Avenue
Dallas, TX 75203
(214) 943-8262
Maintains a large selection of books, posters and related products manufactured by people of color.

Shrine of the Black Madonna Bookstore
Attn: Anika Sala
5309 M. Luther King, Blvd.
Houston, TX 77021
(713) 645-1071
A vast selection of books, cards, posters, gifts and items reflecting Africentric creativity.

U.S. VIRGIN ISLANDS
Education Station Limited
Attn: Latifah
no. 14 Nisky Center
St. Thomas, VI 00802-1103
(809) 776-5433
Fine selection of children's books, games and educational materials with emphasis on the Afro-American/Multi-Culture experience.

Father & Son - photograph
Pat Davis (Courtesy Grinnel Gallery)

GENERAL LISTING

ALABAMA
Mahogany Books & Gifts
(Fairfield)   (205) 923-1624

ARIZONA
New Horizon Enterprises
(Glendale)   (602) 937-7732

ARKANSAS
Mainstreet Bookstore
(Little Rock)   (501) 375-5359

CALIFORNIA
African American Art
(San Jose)   (408) 272-3885

African Reflections
(Oakland)   (510) 420-7042

Alkebulan
(Oakland)   (510) 601-8358

Black & Latino Multicultural Book Center
(Pasadena)   (818) 792-0117

Cody's Books, Inc.
(Berkeley)   (510) 845-9095

General Store Co-Op Univ. of CA, San Diego
(La Jolla)   (619) 534-3167

Global Village
(Santa Monica)   (800) 955-4562
(213) 459-5188

House of Pride
(Pomona)   (714) 620-9022

Kilimanjaro International
(Los Angeles)   (213) 290-0685

Marcus Books
(San Francisco)   (415) 346-4222
(415) 652-2344

Our Learning Tree
(Rialto)   (714) 873-5933

Rising Sun Enterprises
(Tuston)   (714) 838-2114

Samuel's Gallery
(Oakland)   (510) 452-2059

Smith-Wynn Enterprise
(San Jose)   (408) 292-3157

COLORADO
Hue-Man Experience Bookstore
(Denver)   (303) 293-2665

Tattered Cover Book Store
(Denver)   (303) 322-1965

The Chinook Bookshop
(Colorado Springs)   (719) 635-1195

CONNECTICUT
Black Family Cultural Exchange
(Stamford) (203) 661-7332

Somba Bookstore
(Hartford)   (203) 728-5291

Zuri Art & Books
(Bridgeport)   (203) 338-1037

DELAWARE
Haneef's Bookstore
(Wilmington)   (302) 656-4193

Sealand Gallery
(Wilmington)   (302) 475-6380

DISTRICT OF COLUMBIA
Amandla Now
(Washington)   (202) 508-1960

Jewels of Aton
(Washington)   (202) 328-6003

Kobos
(Washington)   (202) 332-9580

Pyramid Bookstore
(Washington)   (202) 328-0190

Seven Powers of Africa
(Washington)   (202) 667-0681

Shades of Indigo
(Washington)   (202) 526-0516

Washington Cathedral Bookstore
(Washington)   (202) 537-6269

FLORIDA

African Imports
(St. Petersburg)   (813) 864-3070

Amen-Ra's Bookshop
(Tallahassee)   (904) 681-6228

Beekon's Cultural Effects
(Miami)   (305) 693-2542

Journey to Africa, Inc.
(Miami)   (305) 573-8981

Montsho Books, Etc.
(Orlando)   (407) 649-8881

GEORGIA

Ambasa Gift Shop
(Augusta)   (404) 738-4601

Charis Books & More
(Atlanta)   (404) 524-0304

First World Bookstore
(Atlanta)   (404) 758-7124

Hamilton's Bookstore
(Augusta)   (404) 722-1301

Isis & Osiris Bookstore
(Athens)   (404) 549-8469

Kujichagulia Foods
(Atlanta)   (404) 758-9479

Rhas' Afrikan Connection
(Scottsdale)   (404) 292-5114

ILLINOIS

African American Book Center
(Chicago)   (312) 651-9101

Afro-Am Distributing Co. Inc.
(Chicago)   (312) 791-1611

Afrocentric Bookstore
(Chicago)   (312) 939-1956

Cultural Learning Tree
(Evanston)   (708) 328-3949

KANSAS

Books For Growing Minds
(Manhattan)   (913) 776-7366

Cultural Expressions
(Kansas City)   (913) 321-4438

LOUISIANA

Side by Side Bookstore
(Lafayette)   (318) 233-1023

MARYLAND

African World Book Wholesalers
(Baltimore)   (301) 728-0877
(410) 523-2705

Asabi International
(Baltimore)   (410) 383-3437
(301) 323-2355

Black Berry
(Hyattsville)   (301) 986-1200

Everyone's Place
(Baltimore)   (301) 728-0877

Hawa Outlet
(Silver Spring)   (301) 587-2985

Insights
(Silver Spring)   (301) 871-6680

Pyramid Books
(Hyattsville)   (301) 559-5200

MASSACHUSETTS

African-American Books
(Springfield) (413) 785-5285

A Nubian Notion, Inc.
(Boston) (617) 442-2622

Caribbean Creations
(Cambridge) (617) 354-2406

The Great Black Art Collection
(Boston) (617) 825-8875

MICHIGAN

African Studies Center Michigan State University
(E. Lansing) (517) 353-1700

A.M. Bookworld
(Detroit) (313) 963-9740

Borders Book Shop
(Ann Arbor) (313) 668-7652

Bronner's Christmas Wonderland
(Frankenmuth) (517) 652-9931

The Cleage Group, Inc.
(Southfield) (800) 325-6524
(800) 325-6025

Hope College Hope-Geneva Bookstore
(Holland) (616) 394-7833

MINNESOTA

St. Martin's Table
(Minneapolis) (612) 340-1463

Uhuru Books
(Minneapolis) (612) 721-7113

MISSISSIPPI

G & G Connections
(Gulfport) (601) 896-8212

Office of Youth Ministry
(Jackson) (601) 366-4452

MISSOURI

Akbar's Books & Things
(St. Louis) (314) 962-0244

Little Africa
(St. Louis) (314) 621-8180

Progressive Books
(St. Louis) (314) 721-1344

Reflections of Ebony
(Kansas City) (816) 921-9644

NEVADA

Native Son Books
(Las Vegas) (702) 455-7316
(702) 647-0101

NEW JERSEY

African House Bookstore
(Jersey City) (201) 433-0191

African Village
(Irvington) (201) 373-2520

Aisha's Gallery
(Montclair) (201) 509-0930

Amistad Gallery
(Piscataway) (201) 823-5580
(908) 752-3588

Bookstore & Co.
(East Orange) (201) 674-1508

Bridges Book Center
(Rahway) (908) 381-2040
(908) 381-4768

Chocolate Huggables
(Montclair) (201) 744-5972

Culture Shock Enterprises
(Newark) (201) 373-3161

Cultural Shocks & Foreign Accents
(Irvington) (201) 373-3161

The Globe African Fashions
(Lakewood) (908) 364-5179

The New Nubou Collection
(Neptune) (908) 775-3298

Positive Images
(Marlton) (609) 9338946
Hm (609) 985-2837

Professional Art Shop
(Elizabeth) (908) 355-8505

Sterling Creations
(Plainfield) (908) 668-7725

Sunrise African Gift Shop
(Newark) (201) 504-9621

Upside Up Art Shoppe
(East Orange) (201) 674-1840

Your Garden of Paradise in America
(Newark) (201) 648-0076

NEW YORK

A & B Books
(Brooklyn) (718) 596-3389

All Day Sunday
(Rochester) (716) 546-3680

Amen Ra & Isis Associates
(New York City) (212) 316-3680

American Museum of Natural History Museum Gift Shop
(New York City) (212) 769-5731

Apercu Gallery
(Brooklyn) (718) 624-5496

Awareness Mart 125
(New York City) (212) 749-5604

Bank Street Bookstore
(New York City) (212) 678-1654

Black Books Plus, Inc.
(New York City) (212) 749-9632

Black Mind Book Boutique
(Brooklyn) (718) 774-5806

Boys & Girls Club of America
(New York City) (212) 351-5900

Cushite Christian Books
(Uniondale) (516) 485-7919

D & J Book Distributors
(Laurelton) (718) 949-5400
(718) 776-8926

Dee's Card & Wedding Service
(New York City) (212) 281-5125

Diana's Card Shop
(Brooklyn) (718) 693-2950

Elimu Bookstore
(New Rochelle) (914) 654-0813

Empire Batist Bookstore
(New York City) (212) 289-7628

Friends for Long Island's Heritage Museum Gift Shop
(Old Bethpage) (516) 572-8415

Gifts on Parade
(Brooklyn) (718) 284-4212

Grand View Imports
(Brooklyn) (718) 693-3410

Harambee Books & Crafts
(Buffalo) (716) 866-1399

Headstart Books & Crafts
(Brooklyn) (718) 469-4500

Here Comes The Dawn
(Hempstead) (516) 486-0447

Kitabu Kingdom
(Rochester) (716) 328-1588

Knowledge Industries, Inc.
(Brooklyn) (718) 858-5050

Lady Alma's Cards & Gift Boutique
(Brooklyn) (718) 789-1905

Light & Dark Botanica
(Yonkers) (914) 969-6717

Mahogany Exchange
(Buffalo) (716) 885-0372

Ms. Print Plus
(St. Albans)   (718) 712-2300

Medger Evers College
Awareness Communication
Bookstore
(Brooklyn)   (718) 270-6409

Nkiru Books
(Brooklyn)   (718) 783-6306

Pan African International
(Hempstead)   (516) 481-5642

Personal Notes by Jo Jo
(Laurelton)   (718) 527-5673

Royal Collage Afrique
(Mount Vernon)   (914) 668-3707

Schomburg Center For
Research in Black Culture
Gift Shop
(New York City)   (212) 491-2200

Source International Tech.
Corp.
(Bronx)   (718) 378-3878

The Baobab Tree
(New York City)   (212) 926-0027

Sudan Jewelers
(New York City)   (212) 677-3930

Sunset Card Shop
(New York City)

Tents of Kedar
(Brooklyn)   (718) 783-6638

That Old Black Magic
(White Plains)   (914) 328-7212

The Studio Museum in
Harlem
(New York City)   (212) 864-4500

Twanya-Kamlon
(W. Hempstead)   (516) 292-6634
(212) 283-1472

Unity Book Center
(New York City)   (212) 242-2934

NORTH CAROLINA
Ashwani
(Charlotte)   (704) 375-7267

Concerned Citizens of Tillery
c/o Tillery Casket Co.
(Tillery)   (919) 826-3244

D.P. Unique Greetings
(Raleigh)   (919) 929-3939
(919) 779-2278

Freedom Books
(Raleigh)   (919) 835-5269

Y.M.I. Cultural Center
(Asheville)   (704) 252-4614

OHIO
Abdul African Arts
(Dayton)   (513) 277-6010

African & Islamic Books Plus
(Shaker Heights)   (216)
921-5181

Black Art Plus
(Columbus)   (614) 469-9980

Little Professor Book Center
(Cincinnati)   (513) 671-9797

Mar-Chris Toys & Gifts
(Cincinnati)   (513) 271-7502

Okoh Imports & Designs
(Kent)   (216) 677-5004

Something Kind of Different
(Girard)   (216) 759-6832

Yours Truly Greetings
(University Heights)   (216)
587-0702

PENNSYLVANIA
Baryeah Import
(Philadelphia)   (215) 223-3559

Chosen Image Art Gallery
(Philadelphia)   (215) 276-3200

Coffee & Cream Gallery
(Pittsburgh)   (412) 362-9882
(412) 362-4112

Hakim's Bookstore
(Philadelphia)   (215) 474-9495

House Kuumba
(Philadelphia)   (215) 438-4461

Khalil's Books & Cultural Shop
(Coatsville)   (215) 384-3082

Know Thyself Bookstore
(Philadelphia)   (215) 748-2278

Merchant of Alkebulan
(Philadelphia)   (215) 226-3240

Steven's Hadithi Center
(Philadelphi)   (215) 424-8285

SOUTH CAROLINA
Unique Ideas
(Charleston)   (803) 723-2956

TENNESSEE
Gestine's Gallery
(Memphis)   (615) 526-3126

Something For Everybody
(Memphis)   (615) 327-0370

TEXAS
African Centricity
(Fort Worth)   (817) 535-4280

Black Images Book Bazaar
(Dallas)   (214) 943-0142

Ebony Fine Art Gallery
(Dallas)   (214) 298-4092

Mitchie's Fine Black Art
(Austin)   (915) 757-2136

Nia Gallery
(Houston)   (713) 729-8400

Pan African Connection Bookstore
(Dallas)   (214) 943-0142

VIRGINIA
Eca Associates
(Chesapeake)   (804) 547-5542

Harrison Museum Afri-Amer Culture
(Roanoke)   (703) 345-4818

Liberation Books
(Alexandria)   (703) 684-7750

Smithsonian Instit. Museum Shops
(Newington)   (703) 603-6041

WASHINGTON
Dream Makers
(Tocoma)   (206) 566-0155

Images of Ebony
(Seattle)   (206) 725-5144

Of African Descent
(Seattle)   (206) 328-6217
(510) 268-0247

WISCONSIN
BDG Trade Enterprises, Inc.
(Milwaukee)   (414) 871-1768

The Reader's Choice
(Milwaukee)   (414) 444-9955

U.S. VIRGIN ISLANDS
Curiosity Shop
(St. Thomas)   (809) 774-5055

Education Station Books
(St. Thomas)   (809) 776-3008

First World Kulture
(Christensted, St. Croix)   (404) 758-7124

Suggested Reading List

"Kwanzaa: Origin, Concepts, Practice," by Dr. Maulana Karenga, Kawaida Publications (1977).

"Reaffirmation and Change," ZNkombo, Vol. 5, No. 2 (January, 1976) p. 17-18.

"Black People and the Future - An Interview," Black Books Bulletin, Vol. 4, No. 2 (Summer, 1976) p. 32-49.

"Names for a New People: An Authentic African Namebook, "Kawaida Publications (1975).

"In Love and Struggle: Towards a Greater Togetherness," The Black Scholar, Vol. 6 (March, 1975) pp. 16-28.

"Accent African: Traditional and Contemporary Hairstyles for the Black Woman - 2nd Edition" by Valarie Thomas-Osborne, Col-Bob Associates, Inc. (1982).

"The African American Holiday of Kwanzaa: A Celebration of Family, Community & Culture" by Maulana Karenga, University of Sankore Press (1989).

"Introduction to Black Studies" by Dr. Maulana Karenga, Kawaida Publications (1982).

"To Be Popular Or Smart: The Black Peer Group" by Jawanza Kunjufu, African American Images (1988).

Transformation: A Rite of Passage for African American Girls" by Mafori Moore, Stars Press, 800 Riverside Drive, =4H, New York, N.Y. 10032 (1987).

"LET'S CELEBRATE KWANZAA: An Activity Book For Young Readers" by Helen Davis-Thompson, GUMBS & THOMAS Publishers, Inc. (1989).

"KWANZAA An Everyday Resource and Instructional Guide" by David A. Anderson/SANKOFA, GUMBS & THOMAS Publishers, Inc.

"Kwanzaa, An African American Celebration of Culture and Cooking" by Eric Copage. William Morrow Publishers.

"The Origin of Life on Earth: An African Creation Myth" by David A. AndersonSANKOFA. Sights Productions, Mt. Airy, Maryland, 1992.